SNAPSHOTS OF
AUSTRALIA

SNAPSHOTS OF
AUSTRALIA

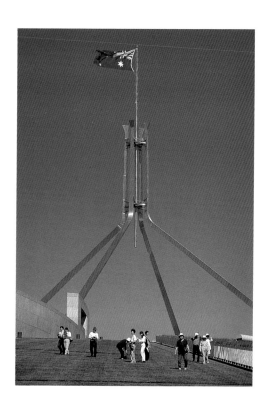

NEW
HOLLAND

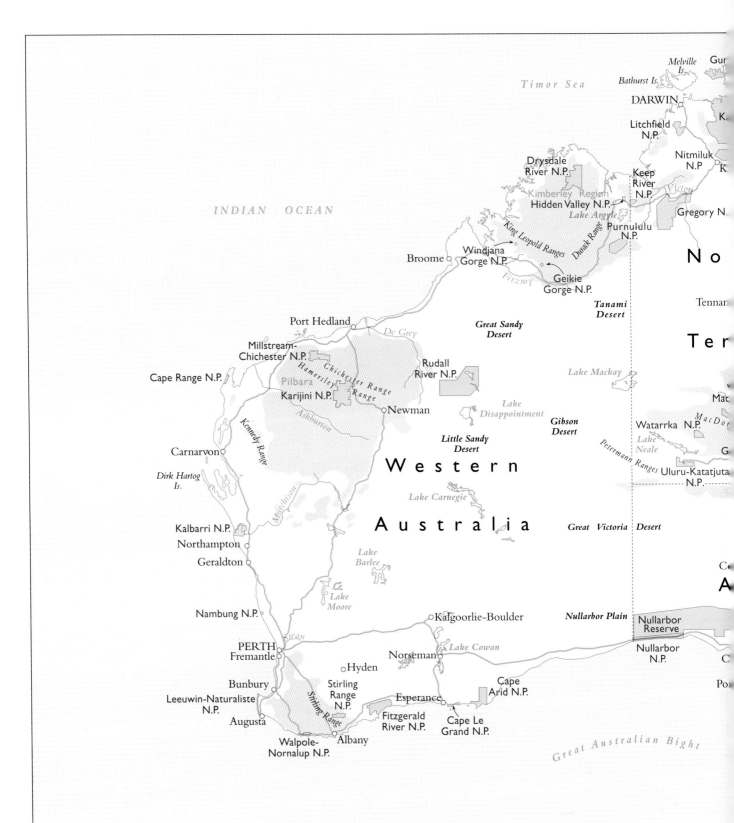

Timor Sea

Melville Is. Gu

Bathurst Is.

DARWIN

Litchfield
N.P.

Nitmiluk
N.P.

K

Drysdale
River N.P.

Keep
River
N.P.

Gregory N.

INDIAN OCEAN

Kimberley Region
Hidden Valley N.P.

Lake Argyle

Purnululu
N.P.

N o

King Leopold Ranges

Durack Range

Broome ○ Windjana
Gorge N.P.

Geikie
Gorge N.P.

Fitzroy

*Tanami
Desert*

Tennar

T e r

Port Hedland ○

De Grey

*Great Sandy
Desert*

Millstream-
Chichester N.P.

Hamersley

*Chichester Range
Range*

Rudall
River N.P.

Lake Mackay

Cape Range N.P.

Pilbara

Karijini N.P.

Ashburton

○ Newman

*Lake
Disappointment*

*Gibson
Desert*

Mac

Mac

MacDo

Watarrka N.P.

*Lake
Neale*

G

Carnarvon ○

Kennedy Range

*Little Sandy
Desert*

W e s t e r n

Petermann Ranges

Uluru-Katatjuta
N.P.

*Dirk Hartog
Is.*

Mitchison

Lake Carnegie

A u s t r a l i a

Great Victoria Desert

Kalbarri N.P.

Northampton ○

*Lake
Barlee*

C

A

Geraldton ○

*Lake
Moore*

Nambung N.P. ○

Kalgoorlie-Boulder ○

Nullarbor Plain

Nullarbor
Reserve

Swan

PERTH
Fremantle ○

Lake Cowan

Norseman ○

Nullarbor
N.P.

C

Po

Bunbury ○

Hyden ○

Stirling
Range
N.P.

Esperance ○

Cape
Arid N.P.

Leeuwin-Naturaliste
N.P.

Stirling Range

Fitzgerald
River N.P.

Cape Le
Grand N.P.

Augusta ○

Albany ○

Great Australian Bight

Walpole-
Nornalup N.P.

N

SOUTHERN OCEAN

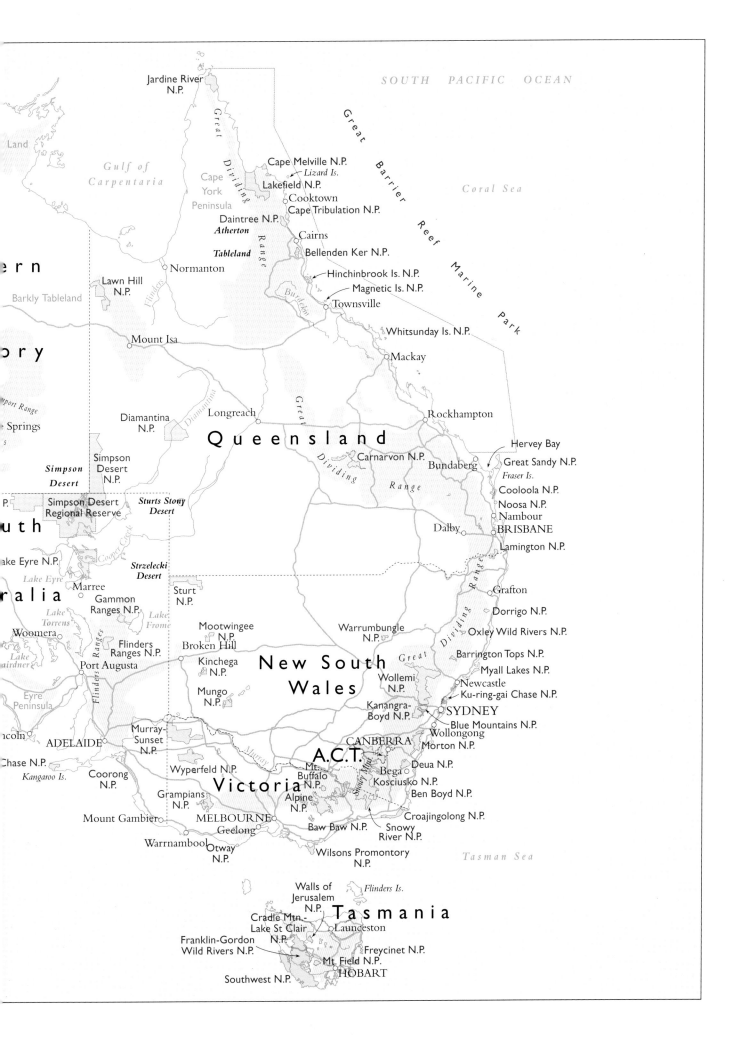

Land

SOUTH PACIFIC OCEAN

Jardine River
N.P.

Gulf of
Carpentaria

Cape
York
Peninsula

Great Barrier Reef Marine Park

Coral Sea

Cape Melville N.P.
Lizard Is.
Lakefield N.P.
Cooktown
Cape Tribulation N.P.
Daintree N.P.
Atherton
Cairns
Tableland
Bellenden Ker N.P.

Hinchinbrook Is. N.P.
Magnetic Is. N.P.
Townsville

Normanton

Barkly Tableland

Lawn Hill
N.P.

Whitsunday Is. N.P.

Mount Isa

Mackay

Great

Rockhampton

Springs

Diamantina
N.P.

Longreach

*Simpson
Desert*

Simpson
Desert
N.P.

Dividing

Queensland

Carnarvon N.P.

Hervey Bay
Great Sandy N.P.
Fraser Is.

Bundaberg

Range

Cooloola N.P.
Noosa N.P.
Nambour
BRISBANE

Dalby

Lamington N.P.

ake Eyre N.P.

Lake Eyre

Marree

Gammon
Ranges N.P.

*Lake
Frome*

Grafton

Dorrigo N.P.

Woomera

Mootwingee
N.P.
Broken Hill

Warrumbungle
N.P.

Oxley Wild Rivers N.P.

Barrington Tops N.P.

*Lake
Torrens*

Flinders Ranges

Flinders
Ranges N.P.

Kinchega
N.P.

New South
Wales

Myall Lakes N.P.

Great

Wollemi
N.P.

Newcastle
Ku-ring-gai Chase N.P.

Port Augusta

Mungo
N.P.

Kanangra-
Boyd N.P.

SYDNEY

Blue Mountains N.P.

lcoln

ADELAIDE

Murray-
Sunset
N.P.

Wollongong
Morton N.P.

A.C.T.
CANBERRA

Deua N.P.
Bega

Chase N.P.

Kangaroo Is.

Coorong
N.P.

Wyperfeld N.P.

Mt.
Buffalo
N.P.

Kosciusko N.P.

Ben Boyd N.P.

Grampians
N.P.

Victoria

Alpine
N.P.

Mount Gambier

MELBOURNE
Geelong

Baw Baw N.P.

Croajingolong N.P.
Snowy
River N.P.

Warrnambool
Otway
N.P.

Wilsons Promontory
N.P.

Tasman Sea

Walls of
Jerusalem
N.P.

Flinders Is.

Tasmania

Cradle Mtn.-
Lake St Clair N.P.

Launceston

Franklin-Gordon
Wild Rivers N.P.

Freycinet N.P.

Mt. Field N.P.
HOBART

Southwest N.P.

AUSTRALIA–A ROUGH DIAMOND?

The 19th-century Irish aesthete Oscar Wilde once threatened to visit Australia to 'do something' about its unruly shape on the map. It's true, the squiggled outline of this great island could resemble a first draft to be perfected later by the Great Cartographer. Australia is shaped, literally, like a rough diamond.

This driest, flattest and smallest continent—the planet's only island continent—drifts just south of the Asian landmass. Home today to around 18 million people, the citizens of this principally immigrant culture have their ancestry in so many other lands that, after Israel, Australia is the most multicultural nation on earth. It wasn't always so, of course.

The first shapers of the rough diamond were the ancestors of Australia's Aborigines who, at least 40 000 years ago, made their island-hopping migrations from south-east Asia. Using fire, they began the transformation of the country's vegetation into that which survives today. Over time, huge expanses of rainforest became the eucalypt forests and plains of today, and megapod animals like giant kangaroos became extinct.

When the first European settlers arrived in 1788, Australia's Aboriginal population was around 300 000. They had developed complex spiritual and kinship systems (often called the Dreaming), spoke some 500 languages and had trading routes across the continent. Aborigines today still number around 300 000, but are now principally town and city dwellers. Contemporary Aboriginal art and music are popular throughout Australia.

During the 17th century, Dutch navigators heading for the Spice Islands of Indonesia frequently bumped into the west coast of Australia—the continent was even known as New Holland. Portuguese and Spanish navigators, lured by the fable of the Great South Land, also explored the area.

It wasn't until Captain James Cook arrived in his barque *Endeavour* that eastern Australia was defined.

Above: *Once a prosperous mining town, Silverton in New South Wales is virtually a ghost town but there is plenty of free parking.*
Left: *A farmhand contemplates life, the outback and a bush camp near Alice Springs in the Northern Territory.*

Cook briefly landed at Sydney's Botany Bay in 1770, whilst on a scientific expedition to Tahiti. He claimed the east coast for Britain, then continued on his way north. A further 18 years passed until England began to use this distant shore (named New South Wales by Cook) as a penal colony for its excess of pickpockets and poachers. Perhaps this is the reason that, even today, some Australians are perceived to have an anti-authoritarian streak even today.

During the 19th century, coastal towns like Melbourne, Brisbane, Adelaide, Hobart and Perth grew gradually. The largest of these, Sydney, was still a penal settlement in 1810 and had a tiny population of only 6156. It was not until 1832 that assisted free settlers started to arrive in New South Wales. The transportation of criminals to New South Wales continued to 1840, and elsewhere in Australia until 1868.

The next major phase in the evolution of the country was the discovery of gold in 1851. The Bathurst district west of Sydney became a magnet for diggers, as did Bendigo and Ballarat near Melbourne soon afterwards. Gold rushes flared around the country, with the last great find being at Kalgoorlie in Western Australia in 1892. Hopeful immigrants with gold fever flocked to Australia from Europe, the Americas and China, rocketing the nation's population to its first million in 1860. For immigrants ever since, Australia has had the lure of a land of opportunity and new beginnings.

All this arriving, digging and building took place in an ancient landscape, one that was already 1000 million years old when the Australian continent broke away (around 50 million years ago) from the supercontinent of Gondwana. From the days of first settlement and even until the 1930s, explorers—some heroic, some quixotic—fanned out along the coasts and across the continent's 7 700 000 square kilometres, discovering new river systems and rich

Above: *A street mural in Tennant Creek in the Northern Territory depicts contemporary Aboriginal culture.*

planting vast tracts of wheat. The hardships these early pioneers endured—isolation, harsh landscapes and an unforgiving climate—helped mould the early Australian character.

In the process of opening up the continent, some animal species such as the so-called Tasmanian Tiger were hunted to extinction, while other unique mammals survived. Marsupials in particular (like kangaroos and koalas) had developed in extraordinary ways on this isolated continent. Other unique creatures to survive the coming of Europeans include the Tasmanian Devil, bandicoot and wombat, plus the world's only egg-laying mammals, the platypus and echidna. Many native birds like emus, kookaburras, lyre birds and cockatoos remain plentiful.

The transformation of an isolated continent into a modern nation began with the declaration of separate British colonies—Victoria, Queensland, South Australia, Western Australia and Tasmania. But it was only with Federation in 1901 that the nation of Australia came into existence; the six colonies became independent of England and joined in a sometimes still squabbling union.

pastoral plains—or at times just disappearing into a waterless, tragic ending. Some searched for a non-existent inland sea, others for fabled lost reefs of gold.

In the wake of the explorers, settlers and mineral prospectors pegged out their territory in an interior with few mountains, but plenty of arid desert. Mount Kosciusko, at 2229 metres, is Australia's highest point. Salt lakes, like Lake Eyre in South Australia, were crossed by teams of camels imported from British India. West of the Great Dividing Range, which runs up the east coast for more than 2000 kilometres, settlers (or squatters) found fertile lands, some establishing huge sheep and cattle stations and

Among those elements that were shaped or reshaped was the English language itself. Novelist Paul Theroux proposes that language is Australia's greatest creative form. Its linguistic playfulness may be attributable to a strong streak of Irish ancestry; certainly there is much rebellious word tweaking and vulgar invention that stamps Australia's as one of the most colourful variations of English. The local vernacular, sometimes known as Strine—which comes from saying 'Australian' through closed

Above: *These vibrant, colourful faces of Australia's youth, with their diverse backgrounds and cultures, have a lot to smile about on a sunny day in Perth.*

Left: *Jervis Bay National Park is part of the Australian Capital Territory, even though it's over 200 kilometres away from Canberra on the New South Wales south coast. Here, children and parents enjoy the fine white sands of Iluka Beach.*

teeth—is not a dialect but a 'slanguage', full of fun and filth, and 'as flash as a rat with a gold tooth'.

If human impact has consistently shaped the Australian landscape, it may be said that, in return, one tiny creature of that landscape—the fly—could have shaped the utterances of those humans. Some claim that the strangled enunciations of Strine arose out of necessity—in the outback one needed to keep one's trap (mouth) shut against the ever-present blowies (blow flies).

In Australia, as elsewhere, the need for national identity has generated a stock of icons and mythical figures: bronzed lifesavers, sporting heroes, outback stockmen, drovers' wives, trench and jungle warfare 'diggers', and also a set of antiheroes. In the 1980s, these bronzed, outback and heroic elements were craftily bundled together in the movie character Mick 'Crocodile' Dundee. However, about five minutes in any Australian city and 10 minutes in a country town will prove to the visitor that Mick Dundee is indeed a myth.

Sport is a national obsession and cricketers, swimmers, runners, surfers, footballers, golfers and tennis players have long waved the Australian flag triumphantly in the international arena. Back home, weekends—if not many weekdays—are transformed into celebrations of sweat, stress and betting. In November each year, the entire nation stops for several minutes during the running of the Melbourne Cup horse race.

The sometimes irreverent and rebellious streak in the Australian character had a prototype in the hero/antihero of the bushranger. During the 19th century the lonely bush roads of the colonies were the preying grounds of armed, mounted highway-men—often escaped convicts or transported Irish rebels—who held up coaches and gold shipments. One bushranger, Bold Jack Donahue, who harassed settlers west of Sydney in the late 1820s, became immortalised in a ballad—which was soon banned by the British authorities. Others had colourful names

Above: *At Beerwah Reptile and Fauna Park in Queensland, a large python considers having quite a large crush on its handler.*

Above: *The wide verandahs of this serene rainforest hideaway in the tropical tourist haven of Cairns, far north Queensland, provide plenty of space for thought.*

like Captain Thunderbolt, Captain Moonlight and Mad Dan Morgan, but by far the most famous (and celebrated) of these 'wild colonial boys' were Ned Kelly and his gang.

Ned considered himself a latter-day Robin Hood and a defender of the oppressed Irish settlers of northern Victoria against their English overlords. During the late 1870s his gang robbed banks and bailed up towns, until in a spectacular siege and shootout at the Victorian town of Glenrowan, he was captured. When Kelly, still only 26 years old, was sentenced to death, he prophetically told the

Above: *The rich red of the rocky cliffs at Gantheaume Point in Broome, Western Australia, is a stunning contrast with the deep blue waters of the Indian Ocean. Low tide reveals footprints believed to belong to a carnivorous dinosaur that lived in the area around 130 million years ago.*

judge, 'I will meet you there.' Ned was hanged in Melbourne on November 11, 1880. The judge died of illness two weeks later.

Railways have played a large part in taming the continent by linking towns separated by tremendous distances. The route of one line, from Adelaide to Alice Springs in central Australia, summarises in a sense the evolution of the continent's transport and communications—from ancient nomadic foot trails to modern diesel locomotives.

In 1862 when Scottish explorer John McDouall Stuart became the first European to cross Australia from south to north, he did so partly by following Aboriginal trading trails and waterholes. Barely 10 years after his epic journey, the 2900-kilometre Overland Telegraph Line was constructed along his route, connecting Adelaide and Alice Springs with Darwin, and then across to Java and the rest of the world. Pioneering Afghan camel teamsters (who brought supplies and mail to lonely outback cattle stations) followed Stuart's trails and the telegraph line; as did, soon after, the track layers of the central Australian railway. Fittingly, the most famous train operating on the Adelaide to Alice Springs line is still known as the Ghan, in memory of the route's early Afghan teamsters.

Particularly during the tough times of the 19th century—in the gold diggings and drought-stricken rural areas—an ethos of mateship (as Australians call it) became inscribed in the national psyche and literature. Mateship encompasses the aspiration of a

Above: *Don't try this one unless the crocodile is completely and utterly stuffed. At Manly Oceanworld in Sydney, this chap gets as close as he'll ever want to be to the slavering jaws of a crocodile.*

fair and equal society, where stoic support and unswerving friendship—sometimes between people who may hardly know each other—are more highly valued than the distinctions of class, cultural heritage, religion or wealth.

How well mateship operates today is like asking how long is a piece of string. In the social landscape of the late 20th century, notions of classlessness are an obvious fantasy. Nevertheless, mateship still counts for much. And, in the country's great egalitarian spirit, should you meet (for example) the Prime Minister on a casual occasion, you wouldn't be expected to address him/her by title, it could simply be 'John' (or 'Kim', or whoever is in power at the time).

Of course, many forces beyond Australia's shores have influenced its evolution as a nation. Australian military expeditions fought in both World Wars, first in the bloody battles of Gallipoli and France and then, from 1939 to 1945, in Europe and Africa, and most vitally in defence of Australian territory against an intended Japanese invasion.

Social stability, political tolerance and general prosperity have been the hallmarks of Australia throughout the 20th century. Institutions like parliamentary democracy (at both federal and state level) are jealously guarded—even if the language of political debate becomes notoriously robust. The New South Wales Parliament is sometimes even known as 'the bearpit'.

More than any other force, immigrants have shaped the Australian society of today: a mix of the old and the new, a minestrone (or gado gado) of optimism and enterprise. Currently, a slight majority of immigrants (from a total of around 90 000 per year) come from Asia. No longer is this an unmistakably Anglo-Saxon-Celtic society, and in the coastal capitals in particular, this multiculturalism is reflected in almost every nuance of life, from cuisine and cinema to intermarriage patterns and mass media programming. Nevertheless, the dominance of American popular culture is also evident, having displaced an earlier dominance by British culture.

In a continent that stretches 3200 kilometres from north to south and 4000 kilometres from east to west, there's almost no limit to the variety of experiences possible. The ochre interior may be home to anyone or everything from wild camels and eccentric prospectors to Aboriginal groups, but most of the population still clusters in the cosmopolitan cities and towns on the south-eastern coast.

In this sometimes unruly, often highly cultured society, subgroups have flourished. They range from nomadic surfers to 'ferals' and greenies, from resolute rednecks to genteel bowls-playing retirees. In all they are the diamonds, polished or rough, who continue to shape, and be shaped by, the largest, roughest, diamond of them all, Australia.

This is a continent of anomalies for beyond its grandeur, there is absolute eccentricity. Perhaps more essential than this is a quality valued by Australians from all walks of life: a spirit of place. The snapshots of this book are an album of that spirit.

Above: *A very popular way of enjoying Queensland's Fraser Island is to take a four-wheel-drive vehicle for a ride along the sands of Seventy Five Mile Beach. Minor obstacles like creeks, washouts and dingoes can turn a ride into a flip, such as with this briefly brand-new vehicle.*

Left: All this and lunch too: sun umbrellas at the forecourt restaurant of Sydney Opera House, the harbour all around and a view of the Sydney Harbour Bridge. Sydney loves its harbour, gazes incessantly in its blue mirror—and has harbourside housing prices to match its beauty.

Top: In the desert of far western New South Wales is an oasis, Broken Hill. Its red earth, blue skies, enormously rich mines and a cast of outback individualists create a distinct local culture. Its most faithful chronicler is resident painter, Pro Hart.

Above, centre: Australian road signs can survive pot-shots, sun and storm and live to a grand old age. These two, pointing to outback homesteads (H.S.), with their distances still stated in miles, have lasted some 30 years after Australia went metric.

Above: The surfboat crew from Sydney's Narrabeen Beach practises on the smooth waters of nearby Pittwater before facing the real thing in the pounding surf.

Top: Bondi Beach is Sydney's most famous pleasure pitch—sand, svelte bodies, endless waves and ice-creams. The name of this beach is believed to stem from the Aboriginal word 'boondi', meaning 'sound of waves breaking on the beach'.

Above: For the aerially inclined, several large ramps have been constructed on the Esplanade at Bondi Beach. Cyclists and roller bladers compete with skateboarders to see who can perform the most death-defying jump.

Left: Near Mt Victoria—in the state of Victoria—the jutting rock formations known as the Balconies preside over the wilderness ridges of the Grampians National Park.

Left: With a 36 700-kilometre coastline, Australia's marine life has plenty to hang on to. The sea lion seen here at Point Labatt on South Australia's Eyre Peninsula is a member of the only mainland colony of sea lions.

Below: Koalas survived the initial trauma and upheaval caused by European settlement, and now these protected animals have special refuges and even hospitals, such as the Billabong Koala Breeding Centre at Port Macquarie on the central north coast of New South Wales.

Bottom: Tasmania usually hosts a fleet of fishing vessels at the historic Constitution Dock in Hobart, but the main party event of the year is the arrival, in late December, of the Sydney to Hobart Ocean Yacht Race fleet.

15

Above: Sweet tooth? Despite their gap-toothed appearance, this row of giant sugar silos at Mackay spells export wealth for the surrounding 'cane cockies' (sugar farmers), whose farms cover thousands of hectares.

Opposite, bottom: Perth's Swan River both drains and entertains the city. Here, powerboats rip along the river—scaring the feathers off any of its namesake black swans that might be gliding past.

Right: Perth, the ever-building capital of Western Australia blooms with money every time there is a new mineral boom in the state. The wildflowers in the city's Kings Park are ultimately more regular, and colourful, in their spring exuberance.

Above: Coober Pedy in outback South Australia is home to a community of opal miners. The landscape is a lunar field of mullock heaps, ancient trucks, and extraction equipment and, thousands of excavation shafts. Not surprisingly, the name Coober Pedy derives from an Aboriginal term for 'white man's hole in the ground'.

Opposite: The Tanunda area in South Australia's Barossa Valley turns rain water into wine, with a little assistance from rich soil, clean air and quality vines planted by early European settlers.
Right: Forget the computers, helicopters and futures markets—cattle mustering still needs a good horse and rider team to get the job done.

Right: A Northern Territory farm-hand gets hot and dirty having a go (yet again) at that never-ending Australian outback farm task, mending the fences.

Below: Around 360 kilometres north of Alice Springs in the Northern Territory are the Devils Marbles, a spectacular cluster of massive granite boulders which Aborigines believed were once the eggs of the legendary Rainbow Serpent.

Opposite, top: Brisbane, the capital of Queensland, reflects upon its sunny good fortune in the not-always-clear waters of the Brisbane River.

Opposite, bottom right: In a bushfire-prone continent, this Northern Territory roadside sign, featuring the frill-necked lizard, says it all.

Opposite, bottom left: At Beerwah on Queensland's Sunshine Coast, a wildlife park ranger and her favourite reptile make a fashion statement.

Above: The former ghost town of Silverton (outside Broken Hill in far western New South Wales) values its 19th-century cottages, churches, pub and courthouse. All of them are carefully preserved as props and scenery for the scores of outback-theme movies and advertisements filmed in this area.

Opposite, top right: A dingo pup at Whyalla's wildlife sanctuary. The dingo is a comparatively recent arrival in Australia, brought here only within the last 10 000 years.

Opposite, bottom: Sydney Harbour is the perfect venue for water festivities and tall ships—especially for the celebrations on January 26, Australia Day.

Right: Coastal Australians realise both the joys and dangers of the sea and the need for trained volunteers such as surf lifesavers and coast guards. This sign at Woolgoolga on the north coast of New South Wales reflects that ethos.

Left: The terrain around Tasmania's Cradle Mountain-Lake St Clair National Park is spectacular, especially in winter. Snows, ice-blue lakes and sparkling peaks make the scenery almost un-Australian— be sure to pack the equivalent of this wallaby's fur coat.

Opposite, top: At the Flagstaff Maritime Museum complex in Warrnambool on the south-west coast of Victoria, actors portray a colourful colonial costume drama whodunnit.

Opposite, bottom right: ...unless you can balance on top of it.

Opposite, bottom left: In Kakadu National Park, ancient rock art galleries portray the spectrum of the Aboriginal experience, from mythical Dreamtime figures to images of early Europeans. Done in the X-ray style unique to the Top End region, the paintings often depict both hunters and their prey, including goannas and wallabies.

Below: The 25-million-year-old limestone pillars known as the Twelve Apostles jut offshore, just off the Great Ocean Road in south-west Victoria. They seem to wade towards the retreating mainland coast.

PLEASE
STAY
BEHIND
THE FENCE

Top left: Pioneer life in the Australian outback was often short and rarely sweet. Many cattle stations, such as Elsey in the Northern Territory— immortalised in the 1908 novel *We of the Never Never*—had their own cemeteries.

Top right: The lookout at West Head in Sydney's Ku-ring-gai Chase National Park is a popular destination for bushwalkers and cyclists. The view of the blue waters of Broken Bay and the isthmus of Palm Beach is superb.

Above: The Aboriginal name for these stunning rock formations is Kata Tjuta, meaning 'many heads'. For most travellers this maze of 36 massive domes is even more spellbinding than their famous neighbour, Uluru.

Right: The Yellow Waters wetlands of Kakadu National Park teem with magpie geese, herons, brolgas, cockatoos and jacanas (known as Jesus birds, because they seem to walk on water). However, a lone crocodile lying along a grassy bank usually steals the show.

Bottom right: The anti-dingo Dog Fence is an effective barricade which separates the fur from the wool, the fangs from the lambs. Its other great achievement is that it's one of the longest fences in the world.

Bottom left: Why do I bear it? This dog's unusual burden is a baby koala—a sight to be seen probably nowhere other than at Brisbane's Lone Pine Sanctuary.

Right: The Big Pineapple at Nambour, near Queensland's Sunshine Coast, is an early example of what seems to be an Aussie tourist industry fetish—if a region produces a lot of something, there's likely to be an enlarged version to explore.

Opposite, top: Separated from the rest of the country by the expanse of the Nullarbor Plain, Perth is one of the most remote cities in the world. Also a symbol of Australian prosperity and mineral wealth, Perth has long been the destination for ambitious immigrants seeking their fortunes.

Opposite, bottom: In the middle of nowhere, there's usually a brown dog, a ute truck and a pub. At the William Creek pub, west of Lake Eyre in central South Australia, you can buy a T-shirt as you sink your tinnie (of beer).

Bottom right: Dingo fences, tick gates and fruit fly-free regions (such as South Australia): one part of the continent is always on guard against contagion from some other part.

Bottom left: Wherever there's water in Australia, someone's sure to have a sailboat, although the degree of skill of some sailors may be another matter. Putting out at Coffin Bay (in South Australia) gives pause for thought.

Left: The sun retires for another day beyond the palms of Darwin's Fanny Bay and into the opalescent blues of the Timor Sea. No other capital city in Australia can match the flamboyance of Darwin's daily sunset show.

Below: The point waves of Bells Beach near Torquay, Victoria play host each year to the world's longest-established professional surfboard riding contest, the Bells Beach Easter Classic.

Bottom right: Broken Hill, a land of giant skies and dust-blackened miners, has a strong creative tradition. Inspired by the outback (or by the endless babble of its local characters) a group of sculptors invited from all over the world laboured for months on a windy hilltop overlooking the desert. The result is a series of chiselled homages known as the Sculpture Symposium.

Bottom left: A fishmonger at Sydney Fish Markets doing what he does best, mongering the day's fish catch.

Opposite, bottom: Mengler Hill Lookout near Tanunda overlooks South Australia's Barossa Valley, the country's premier wine-producing region. The vineyards here were established by German immigrants as far back as 1839.

Opposite: Where better for a hot-air balloon fiesta than Canberra, seat of Australia's Federal Government? Balloon enthusiasts love to take part in this colourful annual festival.

Top: Young cricket fans at a Perth oval vie for their hero's autograph. Cricket is Australia's greatest sports passion—along with horse racing, surfing, football (four different codes), swimming, athletics, motor racing, skiing, fishing...

Centre: Giant waves crash onto the coast near Carnarvon in northern Western Australia and explode through blowholes, sometimes spraying up to 20 metres into the air.

Below: A classic Queenslander house near Bundaberg demonstrates the main features of this distinctly tropical Australian design: corrugated iron roof, wide verandahs, timber construction and a floor elevated on stilts for cooling breezes to pass through.

Left: After a hard day's work picking tomatoes near Carnarvon in Western Australia, this picker may well prefer not to have tomatoes with dinner.

Opposite, top: Visitors to Evans Lookout contemplate the majesty, silence and space of the Grose Valley below them in the Blue Mountains just west of Sydney.

Opposite, bottom right: A Perth street performer in a hat that even Dame Edna Everage would have rejected.

Below: At Western Australia's Nambung National Park, the coastal dunes are studded with hundreds of natural sandstone spires which, from the sea, appeared to early mariners as a ruined city. They were originally formed when limestone encrusted around the roots of ancient dune plants.

Left: Canberra, capital of Australia, has grown up around the man-made Lake Burley Griffin. Home to some 300 000 politicians, diplomats, public servants and academics, Canberra looks good from most angles, especially a hot air balloon.

Opposite, top: The main street of Stroud, north of Newcastle in New South Wales, is lined by well preserved late-19th-century buildings including the Post Office which still functions as it did over 100 years ago.

Opposite, bottom right: An actor brings history alive at the Flagstaff Maritime Museum complex at Warrnambool, Victoria.

Opposite, bottom left: Most country towns in Australia have a war memorial—such as this one at Dorrigo, New South Wales—to honour those servicemen and women who died in action on foreign shores.

Below: Inland from Queensland's Sunshine Coast, the unique Glasshouse Mountains jut out of the coastal plain.

Above: At the rocky Gantheaume Point, near Broome in Western Australia, the low tide reveals giant dinosaur tracks thought to be 130 million years old.
Right: Tiny Northampton, near Geraldton in Western Australia, is a classic rural highway town. Northampton's oldest buildings, such as Chiverton House Museum, were built by convicts.
Opposite, bottom: Sydney's Gay and Lesbian Mardi Gras Parade is probably Australia's biggest single spectator event—some 500 000 onlookers watch the street parade of bizarre floats and participants dressed like, well, Priscilla Queen of Absolutely Everything.

Top: Darwin's Mindil Beach markets are the place to be on a Thursday night in the northern capital. Food vendors sell sizzling satays and luscious fruit salads, the sun does its own spectacular sizzle into the sea, and there are plenty of handicrafts for sale. Aboriginal-style wares such as these boomerangs sell well—and they don't come back.

Right: At Brighton Beach on Melbourne's Port Phillip Bay, these colourful private bathing boxes still line a stretch of the beach.

Above: At Bunbury in the south-west of Western Australia, the Dolphin Discovery Centre celebrates a creature loved by many coastal Australians, especially sailors and surfers.

Below: Fishing is Australia's most popular participant sport, and each year a number of rock fishermen lose their lives to rogue waves. Others, usually sightseers and tourists, perish when the turn their backs on turbulent seas.

Right: Paragliding requires one bright nylon wing, a prayer and a good launching cliff (like Sydney's Long Reef Beach)—plus great faith that you're saying the right prayer when you put all your trust in that wing.

Bottom: Near the town of Hyden, 350 kilometres inland of Perth, a 15-metre-high granite wave seems to be about to dump on an unconcerned visitor. The face of this large granite formation has been hollowed out by wind erosion.

Top: Green gold, sugar, is harvested by the hundreds of thousands of tonnes from northern New South Wales to here in Gordonvale, far north Queensland, and beyond.

Right: South Terrace, the 'cappuccino strip' of Fremantle, Western Australia: take shelter from the sun, have a good burst of caffeine, then hop into the yacht race or head back to the rat race.

Above: Guess what this wire gismo is—and you'll win three of them. Hobart's Salamanca Place craft market, located on the shores of the Derwent River, is one of the city's most popular tourist attractions.

Above: Albany, Western Australia's oldest settlement (established in 1826), overlooks the vast harbour of King George Sound. Once an important whaling port, Albany's old whaling station has been converted into a museum called Whaleworld. This historic town also has a number of colonial-era sandstone buildings.

Left: A turn-of-the-century metal lighthouse dominates Wollongong's convict-built harbour. A flotilla of pelicans attracted by the fishing fleet is a constant presence. Wollongong is the third largest city in New South Wales and has the nation's largest steel works at nearby Port Kembla.

Opposite, bottom: Commonwealth Park in Canberra runs beside Lake Burley Griffin; its leafy pathways are perfect for cyclists and strollers.

Opposite: At Mt Carbine, inland from Mossman in far north Queensland, a ghostly, dead gum tree refuses to actually give up the ghost and fall.

Left: Mareeba means 'meeting place of the waters'. This town on the Atherton Tablelands, inland of Cairns, produces an annual tobacco crop worth many millions of dollars. Other mind- and body-altering substances like coffee and tea are also grown, as is the humble potato.

Above: Camels aren't native to Australia, but they're very much at home. First used as pack beasts, then allowed to run free, they've been rediscovered by the tourist industry. A dromedary ride along Broome's Cable Beach at dusk is almost obligatory.

WARNING
REMOTE AREAS AHEAD

THE FOLLOWING PRECAUTIONS ARE ADVISED

• CARRY ADEQUATE FUEL, WATER, FOOD, CURRENT ROAD MAPS, TWO SPARE TYRES
• TWO JACKS, SHOVEL, FIRST AID KIT, TOOL KIT AND TOW ROPE
• DRINK WATER AT REGULAR INTERVALS TO AVOID DEHYDRATION
• TRAVEL AT SPEEDS APPROPRIATE TO ROAD CONDITIONS
• AVOID NIGHT DRIVING WHEN WILDLIFE AND LIVESTOCK MAY BE ACTIVE
• IN THE EVENT OF BREAKDOWN – NEVER LEAVE YOUR VEHICLE
• DO NOT CAMP IN WATERWAYS – FLASH FLOODS CAN OCCUR WITHOUT WARNING
• AVOID WET WEATHER DRIVING – ROADS CAN BECOME DANGEROUS AND IMPASSABLE
• KEEP FRIENDS OR RELATIVES INFORMED OF YOUR OUTBACK TRAVEL ITINERARY

FOR ROAD CONDITION INFORMATION PHONE (08) 11633

Opposite, top: As this pair of young blossom pickers near Townsville demonstrates, almost everything grows superbly when nourished by the combination of north Queensland's rich soils and buckets of sunshine—and buckets of rain.

Left: The Rocks area of Sydney Harbour never looks better than when it's dressed in tall ships of the sort that once crowded its docks. This replica of Captain Bligh's Bounty is as at home today as it might have been in 1789.

Below: Literally an old warhorse, this World War II truck has lived through numerous reincarnations. These days it hauls mullock to the crushing battery at a gold mine known fittingly as Gun Alley.

Opposite, bottom right: Advisory signs are vital, warning travellers of the total lack of water, fuel or habitation that may lie ahead of them in the outback. Crocodiles, floods, marine stingers, king waves—Australia can be a dangerous place if you don't read the signs.

Opposite, bottom left: After a hard day's hovering, this tourist Hovercraft settles to earth for a rest at dusk near Darwin's Casino.

Opposite, top left: Just offshore from Perth is a small island named Rottnest—Dutch for 'rat's nest'. The first Europeans to land here mistook the island's quokkas—small marsupial relatives of the kangaroo—for rats. Today, this island is Perth's offshore playground: there are no cars, just bicycles, and a pub called the Quokka Arms.

Above: Almost sacred turf, the genteel green of Bradman Oval at Bowral in the Southern Highlands of New South Wales is where the cricketing genius of batsman Sir Donald (The Don) Bradman was honed in the 1930s.

Left: Giant anthills are common throughout the northern parts of Australia, especially around Kakadu National Park in the Northern Territory.

Opposite, bottom: The train arrived, but the gold departed. An old railway station at Pine Creek, south of Darwin, recalls the optimistic 1880s when a local gold strike was in full flush.

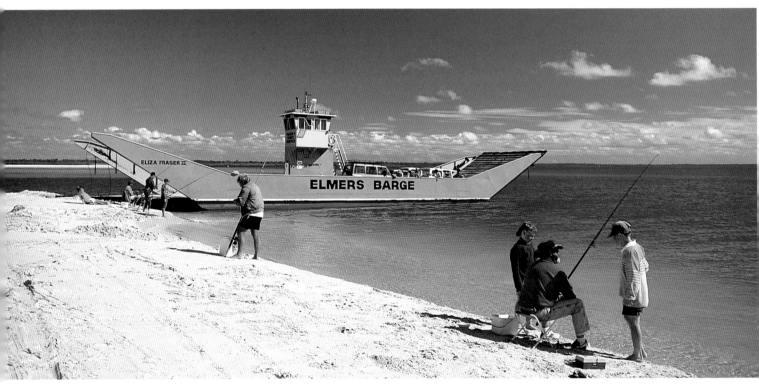

Previous pages: Like massive, mechanical tumbleweeds, rolled bundles of chaff lie in the wake of the harvesting machines on the wheatfields of Northampton, Western Australia.

Top: Fangs for the memory. After a lifetime of shark hunting at Hervey Bay, Queensland, Vic Hislop has turned his hand to commemorating our fascination for sharks of all kinds.

Opposite, top: Not so much outlaws as in-laws, for several decades this group of bikers has dominated a section of Darlinghurst Road's footpath in Kings Cross, Sydney. Many of them are now grandparents who support local issues, and have organised a protest for their local hospital when it was under threat.

Opposite, bottom: The spectacular Sydney Opera House, perching on Bennelong Point in the middle of Port Jackson (Sydney Harbour to the world), fills its voluptuous sails with sunlight and self-confidence.

Above: Inskip Point near Rainbow Beach on the Queensland's Sunshine Coast is the main loading site for the vehicle barges that travel back and forth to nearby Fraser Island, the world's largest sand island.

Top right: Seal of approval—Neptune Coral Cave in Queensland's Hervey Bay, always offers the chance for a slightly fishy romance.

Bottom right: The Herbig Family Tree, said to be 500 years old, is found at Springton, inland from Adelaide. Pioneer Johann Herbig brought his new bride to live in this hollowed-out red gum in 1858. At least one of his 16 children was born within the tree.

Below: This is the stuff of desert dreams. At Coober Pedy in the South Australian outback, miners spend their days—and years—burrowing for a handful like this: $180 000 worth of opal.

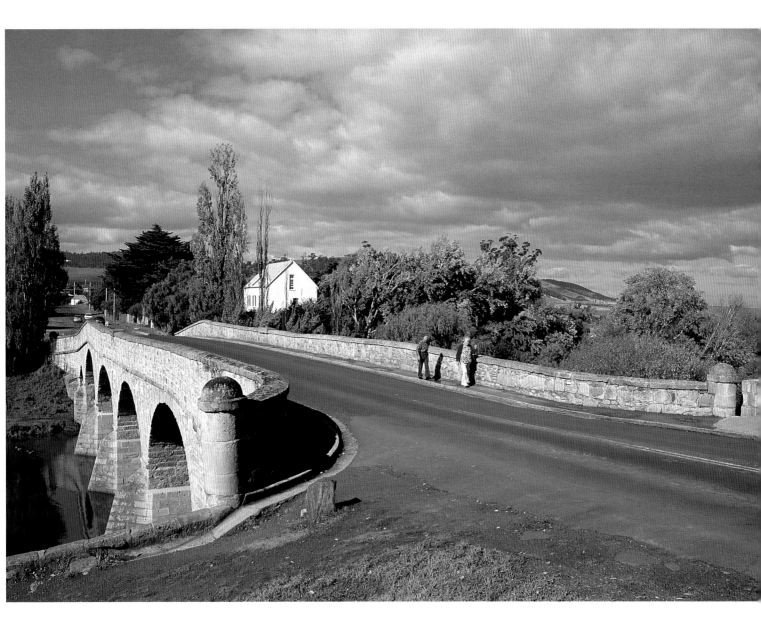

Above: After the Sydney Harbour Bridge, Richmond Bridge in Tasmania is probably the most photographed bridge in Australia. Built in 1823, this fine, convict-built, sandstone structure is the oldest bridge in the country,
Left: This bristling signpost in Mount Isa, central Queensland, can tell you where to go in about 40 different ways.

Opposite, top: Last minute checks to a hang-glider before launching from the cliff-top at Sydney's Long Reef.
Left: Four-wheel-drive vehicles are hugely popular in Australia. Well-graded unsealed roads in most places (such as here at Millstream-Chichester National Park in Western Australia) mean that two-wheel-drive will suffice—until the rains come.
Bottom right: In Marree, outback South Australia, a wooden camel commemorates the camel trains that used the town as a staging post last century and during the first decades of this century.
Bottom left: Of all the introduced animal species in Australia, the camel is one of the least harmful because of its soft-pad foot, as opposed to the hard hooves of most other large animals. Now roaming wild in the centre and the northwest of the continent, feral camels are an occasional road hazard.
Opposite, bottom: With falling wool prices and a depressed rural economy, some farms have moved into tourism, offering homestay accommodation and demonstrations of farm life. At Silver Hills Outback Resort in Queensland, sheep ready for shearing line up to be undressed in front of an audience.

Below: One of Australia's great national pastimes—relaxing on the beach in a deckchair, reading a book, dozing off in the sun...

Right: The most famous sight in Eucla (near the Western Australia–South Australia border) keeps threatening to disappear entirely. It is an old telegraph station, long ago engulfed by sands blown in from the Great Australian Bight.

Opposite, bottom right: Broome, Western Australia, once had over 300 luggers diving for pearls and was home to Malay, Filipino, Chinese and Japanese diving crews. Some 900 Japanese are buried in Broome's cemetery; their ghosts come alive each August during the Shinju Matsuri Festival of the Pearl.

Opposite, bottom left: At Sovereign Hill historic village, near Ballarat in Victoria, the colonial British soldiers are rather less menacing than they were during the region's gold rushes of the 1850s and 1860s.

Bottom: Beulah is the name of this little town on the Henty Highway in central western Victoria. Small as it may be, it still dwarfs nearby West Beulah.

Top left: The Royal Flying Doctor Service base at Broken Hill in far western New South Wales cares for the medical needs of outback people over a 640 000-square-kilometre area. Its services consist of emergency call-outs and regular visits to isolated homesteads and communities.

Opposite: The Kuranda Scenic Rail train leaves from Cairns station each morning and climbs 300 metres through 15 tunnels to the village of Kuranda. The 1891 rail line traverses sugarcane fields, ravines and the spectacular Barron Falls, before arriving at its destination.

Bottom: The town of Grafton on the New South Wales north coast is famous for its purple jacaranda trees and the broad Clarence River, seen here in unusually mirror-like conditions.

Centre left: Sydney's Royal Randwick racecourse, headquarters of the Australian Jockey Club, is a beautiful track. It is said that the only way to win money on horses is by following them with a shovel—as a trackside sage once said, 'The punt giveth and the punt taketh away'.

Left: The beachside Esplanade Hotel, Fremantle, Western Australia—a prime address at which to sink a cool beer.

Opposite, top: Thanks to the Ord River Scheme—an ambitious project to harness the monsoon rains for irrigation projects—thousands of hectares of crops have been planted around Kununurra in north-west Western Australia. Here, watermelon pickers reap the soil's harvest in the bright sunshine.

Opposite, bottom right: The New South Wales south coast town of Bega is traditionally renowned for rich dairy produce—cheese in particular. Now an important administrative and commercial centre, Bega's domestic architecture is a rich reminder of its early history.

Below: The main—if not only—attraction for settlers in Coober Pedy, South Australia, is that white opals are found here in larger quantities than anywhere else on earth. The searing summer heat means that many of the town's 2000 residents live underground. Those that build above ground often do so with all the eccentricity for which Coober Pedy is famous.

Opposite top: Three strong women of Coober Pedy excavated this abode; one of them now lives in it and simply calls it 'Faye's underground home'.

Right: Cossack, near Karratha on the north-west coast of Western Australia, has long been a ghost town; the one-time pearling port shows a few remnants of its brief existence.

Below: Overlooking the Murchison River in the Kalbarri National Park is this dramatic rampart known as Hawk's Head. Not far from here, in 1629, Australia's first known European residents—albeit very temporary ones—were dumped ashore from a Dutch ship; they were two mutineers from a bloody post-shipwreck rebellion.

Opposite, bottom right: Brunswick Street, Fitzroy, Melbourne is a trend-sensitive gauntlet of cafés, coffee bars, pubs, galleries and fashion stores.

Opposite, bottom left: While waiting for the Fraser Island ferry at Inskip Point, you may need a hot dog or soft drink. The Munchmobile is at your command.

Left: These statues of an Aboriginal family group are found in Wyndham, in far north Western Australia.

Below: Broome's Cable Beach was so named when the original underwater communication cable between Java and Australia came ashore there. Today, the beach with its dusk camel rides, is the focus of Broome's tourist industry.

Right: Monkey Mia on Shark Bay, Western Australia, is one of the world's most photographed places of inter-species contact. Here, watched over by local rangers, wild dolphins swim to the shoreline to be gently stroked by human visitors.

Left: The Bungle Bungle Range in Western Australia is a series of deeply carved sandstone structures, eroded into striped beehive-like domes with valleys of palms, ponds and caves hidden between them. This remarkable region only came to public attention in 1983.

Top: This Harley Davidson rider is about as far away from it all as one can be—at Tennant Creek, a gold and copper mining town around 1000 kilometres south of Darwin.

Above: The Australian outback resonates with tales of eccentricity and endurance. One that is commemorated at remote Halls Creek, Western Australia, is the feat of a Russian miner named Jack who supposedly pushed a friend 350 kilometres to Halls Creek in a home-made wheelbarrow.

Top: Kuranda, inland from Cairns, was once known as 'the village in the rainforest'. Today, this tiny village, overwhelmed by tour coaches and souvenir stalls, still manages to retain much of its charm.

Above: These pelicans at Monkey Mia can't understand all the fuss about a group of slow-learner dolphins who've finally wised up and accepted hand-feeding by humans. Pelicans insist that they've been doing it for centuries.

Left: Kalbarri National Park, Western Australia, encompasses the lower reaches of the Murchison River as it flows towards the Indian Ocean.

Left: The boutiques and restaurants in the inner-Sydney suburb of Newtown are renowned for their off-beat humour.

Below: One of the Australia's most hallowed sports grounds is the Melbourne Cricket Ground. It served as the main stadium for the 1956 Olympic Games and, in 1961, held a world-record crowd of 90 800 when Australia met the West Indian cricket team. Greater passions than the ones stirred by cricket are those for Australian Rules Football, seen here played under floodlights.

Bottom: Along the original (and now disused) line of the Central Australian Railway were whistle-stops that consisted of little more than a water-tank, a pub and a cross-roads for stray camels or cowboys. These places had curious names like Oodnadatta, Birthday and Dodge City. At lonesome Curdimurka, a few traces of the historic railway line remain.

Above: Besides serving thousands of city-bound commuters, Manly Wharf is a popular ferry destination for tourists, with its restaurants and amusement park, nearby Oceanarium, art gallery and famous ocean beach.

Opposite, right: Home to the spectacular Jewel Cave with its limestone encrustations and underground river, Augusta in Western Australia is Australia's most south-westerly town.

Opposite, left: Atherton, the hub of north Queensland's Atherton Tablelands is an honest, down-to-earth rural town. The Crystal Cave is a gallery of crystal wonders from around the world.

Right: The well-known Catalina Restaurant is located in one of Sydney's exclusive waterfront suburbs, Rose Bay.

Opposite: No matter how many there are, Australia will never have enough wildlife sanctuaries for all the kids who love to pat a sleepy kangaroo.

Right: At Dalby in southern Queensland this plaque celebrates the elimination of the Prickly Pear cactus, one of the many introduced species that have wreaked havoc upon Australia's fragile ecology. Now for the rabbits, foxes, cane toads, lantana, feral cats...

Above: With three million people, Melbourne—seen here glittering by night from the Rialto Tower—is Australia's second largest city. It has come a long way since its beginnings when, in 1835, John Batman disobeyed Governor Burke's orders and swapped a parcel of land from local Aborigines for tomahawks, blankets and trinkets.

IN 1925,
PRICKLY PEAR, THE GREATEST EXAMPLE
KNOWN TO MAN OF ANY NOXIOUS PLANT INVASION,
INFESTED FIFTY MILLION ACRES OF LAND IN QUEENSLAND,
OF WHICH THIRTY MILLION REPRESENTED A COMPLETE
COVERAGE. THE DALBY DISTRICT WAS THEN HEAVILY INFESTED.
THE BIOLOGICAL CONTROL INVESTIGATION WAS UNDERTAKEN
BY THE COMMONWEALTH PRICKLY PEAR BOARD,
THE JOINT PROJECT OF THE COMMONWEALTH, QUEENSLAND AND
NEW SOUTH WALES GOVERNMENTS.
EARLY IN 1925, A SMALL NUMBER OF CACTOBLASTIS CACTORUM
INSECTS WAS INTRODUCED FROM THE ARGENTINE BY
ALAN PARKHURST DODD, O.B.E., WHO WAS OFFICER-IN-CHARGE OF
THIS SCIENTIFIC UNDERTAKING. THEY WERE BRED IN VERY
LARGE NUMBERS AND LIBERATED THROUGHOUT THE PRICKLY PEAR
TERRITORY. WITHIN TEN YEARS, THE INSECTS HAD DESTROYED ALL
THE DENSE MASSES OF PRICKLY PEAR.

THIS PLAQUE, AFFIXED BY
THE QUEENSLAND WOMEN'S HISTORICAL ASSOCIATION
ON THURSDAY, 27 TH. MAY, 1965, RECORDS THE
INDEBTEDNESS OF THE PEOPLE OF QUEENSLAND,
AND DALBY IN PARTICULAR, TO THE CACTOBLASTIS
CACTORUM, AND THEIR GRATITUDE FOR
DELIVERANCE FROM THAT SCOURGE.

Right: For decades the Australian countryside was dotted with spindly, wind-driven bore pumps that supplied water for livestock—such as this one at Penong, South Australia. With the electrification of even remote areas, the old windmills are now being replaced by electric pumps.

Bottom: Coogee, on Sydney's southern beaches, is a favourite spot with swimmers who prefer not to set foot in the rough water of open surf. Coogee's Ocean Baths have nurtured generations of swimmers, from early paddlers to veteran lappers.

Below: Going busk at Sydney's Circular Quay. A one-man bush orchestra plays a tune on the back of a saw and a folded gum-leaf.

Above: Port Arthur, Tasmania, is a grim reminder of European Australia's origins as a penal colony. The place was so harsh 150 years ago that many prisoners preferred death to a sentence at Port Arthur. The main penitentiary was built in 1842 as a granary, but ended up housing over 600 prisoners. Nowadays the grounds of the ruins appear like a tranquil park.
Left: Noosa Heads, the main resort town of Queensland's Sunshine Coast, is adjacent to the Noosa River and a beautiful national park coastal forest. Here the crews of surf canoes prepare for an inter-city competition.

Above: In Townsville, Queensland, the sun sinks slowly in the west over a replica of Captain Cook's ship *Endeavour*. Cook's real vessel almost sank slowly in the east when, in 1770, it hit the Great Barrier Reef just off today's Cooktown.

Opposite, top: Some signs are more useful than others—railway crossings can be difficult to see, like this one running through sugarcane fields.

Opposite, bottom: There are many pubs in Australia called 'the National'. Years ago, the National Hotel at Normanton on the Gulf of Carpentaria changed its colour scheme to purple— and soon became famous far and wide as 'the Purple Pub'.

Right: Darwin, capital of the Northern Territory, was destroyed by a cyclone in December 1974. Now entirely rebuilt, this city on the Timor Sea (first established in 1869) has a multicultural population of 75 000 and is seen as Australia's gateway to south-east Asia.

Previous pages: Fishing can be a timeless activity, especially in the peaceful surrounds of Chinaman's Rock, Kalbarri, Western Australia.

Left: At rural Beechworth, Victoria, a rider ambles down Camp Street. In the midst of rolling hill country, this is Victoria's best preserved gold town: 32 of its buildings are classified by the National Trust, including the 1856 Robert O'Hara Burke Memorial Museum. During its gold rush heyday, the town had 61 hotels.

Opposite, top: The MacDonnell Ranges near Alice Springs are almost at the geographical centre of the continent. They shelter a warren of sandy, tree-lined gorges, such as this one in the Simpsons Gap National Park.

Opposite, bottom: A camel on a diet? On the Mall in Rockhampton, on the Tropic of Capricorn, such things don't bother this camel and its drinking partner.

Below: A former Royal Flying Doctor Service plane at the Aviation Museum, located on the site of the first airport in Alice Springs.

Opposite, top: Some places aren't as new as they once were, as this former church in New Norfolk, Tasmania demonstrates.

Left: Famous Hawaiian, Duke Kahanamoku introduced surfboard riding to Australia at Sydney's Freshwater Beach in 1915. Having seen that mortals could walk on water, Australian surfers have remained obsessed since that day. The Duke is honoured by this statue overlooking Freshwater Beach.

Bottom right: The Top End crocodiles don't keep spectators waiting long, especially on Adelaide River, just south of Darwin. Here, a daily jumping crocodile show has the ravenous giants performing jump shots for a quick feed.

Bottom left: There are just too many hats to choose from at Darwin's Mindil Beach markets, including the world-famous Akubra. Made from rabbit fur felt, the Akubra, from the Aboriginal meaning 'headcovering' is popular all over the country.

Opposite, bottom: An old locomotive that once hauled the Adelaide to Alice Springs Ghan train sits forlornly in the desert at Marree, South Australia. The Ghan was so slow that it was known as the train to check your watch by—if it was on time, your watch was wrong. If there were floods, the two-day journey sometimes took up to two months.

Opposite: Pillars of wisdom and stacks of books—the University of Western Australia in Perth.

Top: Derby, on the north coast of western Australia, is the administrative centre for the huge cattle-producing area of West Kimberley. Authorities no longer use this tree, a huge, hollow ancient boab where criminals on their way to face justice in Derby were temporarily imprisoned.

Centre: Behind Queensland's Gold Coast is a fantasy land of theme parks—Warner Bros Movie World, Sea World and Wet 'n' Wild and Dreamworld. You can loop the loop, or be suspended upside down on the 'Wipeout' at Dreamworld, which is like an Australian-oriented Disneyland.

Below: Camels were once the long-haul transport service to Marree, South Australia. They were phased out with the arrival of the Central Australian Railway in the late 1920s, which then died half a century later when the track was moved to the east. Today this desert oasis serves long distance semi-trailers and road trains.

Left: At Tasmania's Dover Harbour, south of Hobart, the morning's catch is unloaded from fishing trawlers—a scene repeated daily around the Australian coast.

Opposite, top: Over 300 pearl luggers worked the north-west coast of Australia during the 1920s, most of them based around Broome. Since plastic buttons, there are no longer scores of luggers at anchor, although a few pearling boats still work the offshore waters.

Opposite, bottom right: Like a Martian's sceptre, the Telstra tower that dominates Canberra's Black Mountain is an enigmatic sight. From its observation decks and revolving restaurant, one can gaze down with attitude on the nation's capital and its rulers.

Below: Uluru—seen here from the west—is the largest monolith in the world. 'Climb to the top and you've got the best possible view of nothing', say the local Mutitjulu Aboriginal people, who prefer that visitors don't climb the rock. At sunset the colour of the rock shifts constantly, from pink to red to mauve.

Top: Road trains are distinctly Australian. These 50-metre-long giants—the wheeled world's equivalent to the centipede—are vital to the inland and the north, hauling massive loads of produce, minerals and livestock. This one at Port Hedland is carrying manganese ore.

Above: Ballarat, in Victoria, was once famous for gold; these days its fame endures in the begonias blooming in its glasshouses.

Left: Longreach in central western Queensland is home to the Australian Stockman's Hall of Fame, which honours the drovers and pioneers who opened up the inland. A dramatic bronze statue in the grounds depicts a 'ringer', an Australian cowboy. Also at Longreach is the original 1922 base and hangar of Qantas Airways.

Right: Lawn bowls seems a tranquil game, but when it comes to the crunch, these genteel players are just as competitive as any other sports fiends.

Below: Echuca, in northern Victoria, used to be famous for its Murray River paddle-wheelers which, laden with cargo and passengers, made the river a busy thoroughfare. Then came the automobile and the railway, followed by the aeroplane. At Echuca, Raverty's Motor Museum preserves at least part of the transport past.

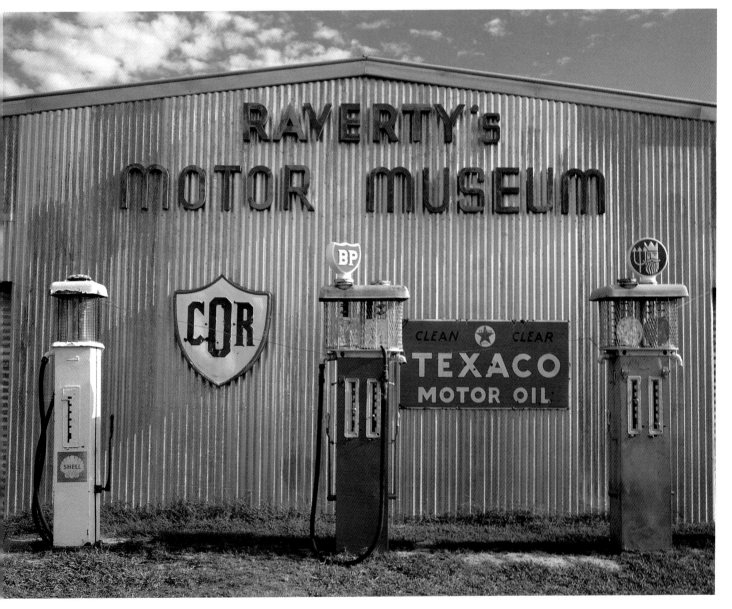

Above: Pirate-explorer William Dampier visited the north-west of Australia briefly in 1799. Little did he realise the wealth that lay nearby in the Pilbara region. Here, iron ore is the new gold; after mining it is freighted by rail to Port Hedland (seen here) for shipping to local or overseas processing plants.

Right: Australia attracts over three-and-a-half-million international tourists each year; on current trends, by the year 2000, annual arrivals will be around five million. After Sydney, one of the most popular destinations is Queensland's Surfers Paradise.

Opposite, bottom: Sydney's corporate walls glow golden in the afternoon sun. A moat of blue waters surrounds the glass-and-girders downtown, beyond which are endless red-roofed suburbs.

Produced and published in Australia by
New Holland Publishers
3/2 Aquatic Drive
Frenchs Forest
NSW 2086
Australia

Publishing General Manager: Jane Hazell
Publishing Manager: Averill Chase
Designer and Typesetter: Arne Falkenmire
Editor: Jacquie Brown
Picture Researcher: Vicki Hastrich
Production Controller: Paula Leavy
Reproduced and printed in Hong Kong

ISBN 1 86436 267 7

PACIFIC TREE FROGS

George Juhasz 2002

First published simultaneously in 2002 in Great Britain, USA and Canada by Tradewind Books Ltd.

tradewindbooks@eudoramail.com § www.tradewindbooks.com

Distribution and representation in the USA by the Interlink Publishing Group § www.interlinkbooks.com

Distribution and representation in the UK by Turnaround § www.turnaround-uk.com

Distribution and representation in Australia by John Reed Books § johnreed@barcode.com.au

Book design by Elisa Gutiérrez

Printed and bound in Canada
10 9 8 7 6 5 4 3 2 1

Cataloguing-in-Publication Data for this book is available from The British Library.

National Library of Canada Cataloguing in Publication Data

Owen, Leslie, 1958-
  Pacific tree frogs

  ISBN 1-896580-42-4

  I. Pacific treefrog. I. Juhasz, George, 1933- II. Title.
QL668.E24O93 2002   597.8'7   C2002-910210-3

Library of Congress Cataloging-in-Publication Data

Owen, Leslie E. 1958-
  Pacific tree frogs / Leslie E. Owen ; illustrated by George Juhasz.
      p. cm.
Summary: Provides a detailed look at one complete year in the life of a Pacific tree frog.
  ISBN 1-896580-42-4 (alk. paper)
  1. Pacific treefrog--Juvenile literature. [1. Pacific treefrog. 2. Tree frogs. 3. Frogs.] I. Juhasz, George 1933- ill. II. Title.
  QL668.E24 O94 2002
  597.8'7--dc21

  2002005399

The publisher thanks the CANADA COUNCIL FOR THE ARTS and the BRITISH COLUMBIA ARTS COUNCIL for their support.

PACIFIC TREE FROGS

Leslie E. Owen ⁊ Illustrated by George Juhasz

Vancouver Boston London

A cool mist swirls upwards from shallow roadside pools. Spring rain splashes into ditches and gullies.

A tree frog stirs beneath the leaf litter. The cold spring rains wake him from hibernation.

This Pacific tree frog (*hyla regilla*) is about the size of an adult finger. He has sticky toepads on his front and back feet which help him climb the tall marsh grasses, cattails, and alder saplings that will be his summer home.

At the pool's edge, the frog climbs a blade of sedge. His skin changes from a light green to a dull tan. Only his black eye stripes never change.

With a deep breath, air fills the frog's vocal sac, just beneath his throat. He calls *reek... reek... reek... reek...* over and over again.

Beneath the leaf litter other male frogs hear the chorus leader's call. Soon the night air is filled with the music of spring.

*H*undreds of Pacific tree frogs call out this song for hours and hours each spring night. They cling to the grass blades and alder saplings, their skin tones matching each plant. In the daytime, they are silent. At night, their songs are loud and beautiful.

*T*he female frogs take longer to wake. Ten days after the chorus leader's first song, the female frogs abandon their winter homes. They plunge into the pools and the male frogs now join them. The chorus leader mates first.

As the female lays her string of jelly-coated eggs, or spawn, the male releases his sperm to fertilize them. The small clumps of eggs are attached to grass, twigs or cattails in the water. This is to keep the spawn from being washed away.

Mating can take two to three weeks. Then the frogs will separate, with each frog finding a territory of its own.

The tree frog is a predator, an animal that hunts for its food. But the tree frog does not search for its prey. Instead, it waits for movement. Then it lunges forward and catches the insect — a moth, a fly, a mosquito — with its long, sticky tongue. The frog does not chew its food, even though it has teeth. It uses the teeth to hold onto the insect and then it uses its eyes to press down and help it swallow the insect whole.

An insect sitting still right beside the frog would be safe. The frog can only see it when it moves.

*T*he spawn which are left in the shallow pools and creeks hatch as tadpoles in about two weeks. They eat the smallest animals in the water, such as fairy shrimp and mosquito larvae. They breathe through their feathery gills, like fish, and swim by moving their very long tails.

These smallest of tadpoles are prey to dozens of other animals. Dragonfly and mayfly nymphs, minnows, sticklebacks, water boatmen, diving beetles, and even other tadpoles eat the tree frog tadpoles.

By the beginning of summer the tadpoles are froglets. Some may still have a tiny nub of a tail. It will be gone by the end of the summer. The froglets are tinier than the tadpoles were, no bigger than a small fingernail. Like all amphibians, the froglets' skin must stay moist. Frogs do not drink water. Their skin is permeable, which means water can pass right through it. The froglets are very delicate, and must stay at the edges of pools and creeks, or they will dry up and die.

Tree froglets are prey to many animals.

coyote   *racoon*

otter

great grey owl

skunk

*B*ullfrogs, green frogs, rough-skinned newts, garter snakes, and great blue herons are some of the other animals that eat the tiny tree frogs.

The adult tree frogs have the same enemies as the froglets. But they are better able to keep themselves safe. They do not dry out as easily as the froglets do, and often will have territories some distance from a pool or stream. Also, the adult frog's ability to mimic its surroundings — called camouflage — is greater, too. In Vancouver, a city in Canada, a gardener once found a red tree frog in her red geraniums!

garter snake

bullfrog

great blue heron

As the days grow shorter, the tree frogs must find winter homes. This is because frogs, like all amphibians, are cold-blooded. Frogs have no way to control their own body temperatures, the way mammals and birds can. Frogs must rely on the sun to keep them warm, and on water and shade to keep them cool. In late autumn, they will return to the leaf litter of the woods, or will dig burrows beneath rocks and tree roots. Their bodies will slow down until it seems they are dead. Then they will sleep until the cold rains of spring wake them up again. This process is called hibernation.

At one time Pacific tree frogs were the most numerous frogs of the west coast of the United States and Canada. Their spring song was heard from the wetlands of British Columbia to the farmlands of southern California. But in the past ten to twenty years, frogs all over the world have been disappearing. While the Pacific tree frog is not on the endangered species list yet, whole colonies of them continue to disappear from the places where they were once abundant.

Tree frogs are disappearing because we are destroying their wetland homes. They need rain-filled spring pools in order to breed. Every time another roadside pool or wooded creek habitat is destroyed more tree frogs cannot breed.

What can you do to help? The best way to help is to adopt a local pool or creek where tree frogs live. Your parents and teachers can help you to write to your town or city council. You can encourage them to set aside wetlands so the tree frogs can breed and live. Scientists now believe that frogs play an important role in telling us if our world is healthy. Wetlands are important because they help keep our drinking water and our air clean. ⁓ If you should catch a Pacific tree frog, or any kind of frog, remember that many provinces and states now require you to own a permit to keep amphibians. Frogs

are great fun to watch and study, but they are very fragile, and you should not keep any wild animal captive for more than a day or two. Catch and release is the very best way to study any wild frog. ૭ *The tree frogs shown in these two pages from left to right are: tropical tree frog, tropical horn frog, tree toad, Amazonian rough-skinned tree frog, Brazilian tree frog, African reed frog, basin tree frog, spring peeper, common poison arrow frog, European pond frog, green poison arrow frog, chorus frog and grey tree frog.*